SAINSBURY'S

Quick and Easy

Cooking for Students

Cas Clarke

Contents

Published exclusively for J Sainsbury plc
Stamford House Stamford Street
London SE1 9LL

by Martin Books
Simon & Schuster Consumer Group
Grafton House 64 Maids Causeway
Cambridge CB5 8DD

First published September 1994
Third impression September 1995

ISBN 0 85941 863 4

©1994 Martin Books

Printed and bound in the UK by Bath Press
Colourbooks
Design: Green Moore Lowenhoff
Photography: Iain Bagwell
Styling: Maria Kelly
Food preparation: Louise Pickford
Typesetting: Goodfellow & Egan Ltd, Cambridge

Pictured on the front cover: Mexican Pork and
Vegetable Casserole (page 56)

Introduction

It is not easy being a student. It may well be your first experience of having to manage for yourself, and amongst the many new skills that you must master are those of budgeting and cooking. Most students quickly discover that their money doesn't go very far!

But money isn't the only problem that you will have to deal with as a student. Many students have to share quite primitive kitchens, having to do without the mod-cons that we are all growing used to – for instance, a microwave oven. Refrigerator space will be at a premium in shared accommodation. Most students do not have access to a freezer and will have only a small locker in which to keep foodstuffs. In a letter I recently received from a current student, she explained that because of problems in their kitchen, 50 students were sharing an oven!

However it is still possible for you to eat a diet which is healthy and low-cost, whilst being quick and easy to prepare. To avoid waste and having to deal with unfamiliar objects, I advocate that canned and dried ingredients, supplemented by inexpensive fresh produce, form the basis of meals for the novice cook. Whenever possible, share cooking with a friend, making cooking cheaper and more enjoyable.

I have tried to keep down the number of items you need as 'storecupboard' stocks. The main items I use are garlic, curry paste, mustard (dry and French), Worcestershire sauce, chilli or hot pepper sauce, coconut milk powder, soy sauce and pesto. As pesto needs to be kept in a refrigerator, it may be necessary to substitute dried Italian herbs (especially if you suffer from light-fingered friends 'borrowing' your food from a communal 'fridge!).

Then as you become more experienced I recommend improving on your finished results by upgrading the ingredients used. Most students, for instance, use a cheap cooking oil for frying. I thoroughly recommend swapping to groundnut or olive oil – not only on health grounds, but because it really does improve the flavour of the end result. Again, most students rely on dried herbs to add variety to their meals, but if finances permit it, I would advocate changing to fresh herbs – the difference is amazing! Students who are lucky enough to be able to buy fresh fruit and vegetables on a regular basis should take advantage of this and use them freely. Fruit and vegetables are excellent value for money and in health terms cannot be bettered, being a good source of fibre and crammed with vitamins and minerals. The World Health Organisation advocates that we try to eat five portions of fruit and vegetables daily. This is not as difficult as it may seem:

consider the times that the average student snacks on crisps or chocolate, and then imagine substituting a piece of fruit instead. Five portions would be no problem!

To increase the amount of fruit and vegetables you are eating, try the following guidelines. Try adding fresh fruit to your breakfast cereal (or dried fruit such as apricots). Mid-morning, have an apple or an orange. Try to have a portion of salad at lunchtime and/or follow lunch with a piece of fruit. Either include some vegetables in your main meal or serve some to accompany it, and you will easily get through five portions a day.

Do try to have a good variety of fruit and vegetables in your diet; if you are including broccoli, carrots, tomatoes, oranges and at least one type of bean, such as peas, green beans or canned beans in your diet, you will not be going far wrong.

All of these recipes are aimed at the complete novice in the kitchen. You will soon learn to open a can and chop up an onion! However, where I have seen many inexperienced cooks come to grief is in their ability to gauge on how high a heat to cook items on the hob. As a rough guide, if it is impossible to get near the frying-pan because of the risk of fire, the heat is too high! Likewise, if there is absolutely no sign of activity in the pan, the heat is too low, or it has been turned off or it was never on in the first place. Most frying activities should quickly produce a browning effect, and, usually, a pleasant smell.

I have given you some idea of how long it takes to cook these recipes, but you will still need to use your own judgement. Cookers do vary! For example, one grill may take only seconds to brown items, whilst another will take several minutes. It is important whilst cooking to keep an eye on how the food is progressing. Is the pan looking suspiciously dry? Is the food cooked through when tested, or does it need a few minutes longer? Also keep tasting as you go. You may prefer your food to be spicier than I have recommended, or you may have certain flavours you dislike: if so, substitute others. You are cooking for yourself – so add the amount of seasoning that you prefer.

Pasta has to be one of the most important foods for students. If necessary, it can be stored in your room; it does not go off; it is cheap; and, if finances are really at rock-bottom, it can even be eaten with just margarine and some seasoning. Pasta is supremely easy to cook. Bring a large pan of water to the boil, add salt if you like, throw in the pasta and within 8–12 minutes it will be ready (the cooking time depends on the variety – the pack will tell you how long you should allow). To test to see if it is cooked, scoop a piece out and try it. It needs to be tender (not soggy) and still with a little 'bite' to it. Drain it immediately and use it straightaway.

Another area to watch is when cooking rice. It is important to keep an eye on rice, as it can quickly go from the point where the water/stock it is cooking in is nearly absorbed, to becoming thoroughly stuck on to the bottom of the pan.

You won't need a lot of expensive cooking equipment, but there are some items you won't be able to do without. The following is a list of what I think is essential equipment.

ABSOLUTELY ESSENTIAL

sharp knife and can opener
(guard these with your life)
set of measuring spoons
measuring jug
wooden spoon
colander
cutlery and crockery

IF NOT PROVIDED

large and small saucepan
frying-pan
casserole dish
chopping board
mixing bowl
cheese grater

Bearing these points in mind, I am confident that anyone can cook. I hope that these recipes will inspire you to prove this to yourself!

RECIPE NOTES

All recipes in this book give ingredients in both metric (g, ml, etc.) and Imperial (oz, pints, etc.) measures. Use either set of quantities, but not a mixture of both, in any one recipe.

All teaspoons and tablespoons are level, unless otherwise stated. 1 teaspoon = a 5 ml spoon: 1 tablespoon = a 15 ml spoon.

Egg size is medium (size 3), unless otherwise stated.

Vegetables and fruit are medium-size unless otherwise stated.

Freshly ground black pepper should be used throughout.

PREPARATION AND COOKING TIMES

Preparation and cooking times are included at the head of the recipes as a general guide: preparation times, especially, are approximate and timings are usually rounded to the nearest 5 minutes.

Preparation times include the time taken to prepare ingredients in the list, but not to make any 'basic' recipe.

The cooking times given at the heads of the recipes denote cooking periods when the dish can be left largely unattended, e.g. baking, and not the total amount of cooking for the recipe. Always read and follow the timings given for the steps of the recipe in the method.

Things on Toast

Students probably resort to 'things on toast' more often than most. Possibly because this requires less effort than actual cooking, but also because bread happens to be one of the staples of the student diet.

However, this type of snack should not be undervalued. If the bread is wholemeal and the topping nutritious, 'something on toast' will fill you up and make a decent contribution to a healthy diet too.

Cheese Toasties

Preparation and cooking time: 10 minutes. Serves 1–2.

I have used a sweet pickle in this recipe but you can use any type you like. I tend to use either sweet pickle or tomato chutney; it is also very good with mango chutney.

4 slices of bread

50 g (2 oz) cheese, grated

1 teaspoon French mustard

2 teaspoons soft margarine

2 teaspoons sweet pickle

❶ Toast the slices of bread on one side.
❷ Mix all of the other ingredients together and then spread them on the toasted side of two of the bread-slices.
❸ Top with the other slices, untoasted-side up.

❹ Toast until brown. Turn the toasties over and brown on the last untoasted side. Serve immediately.

Mushrooms on Toast

Preparation and cooking time: 10 minutes. Serves 1.

I always use chestnut mushrooms for the best flavour, but substitute ordinary white button mushrooms if you prefer.

2 slices of wholemeal bread

2 teaspoons soft margarine

1 teaspoon French mustard

2 teaspoons tomato ketchup

50 g (2 oz) chestnut mushrooms, sliced thinly

❶ Toast the slices of bread on one side.
❷ Mix all of the other ingredients together.
❸ Turn the bread over and toast the other side until the bread is starting to crispen but is not yet brown.

❹ Spread each slice with the mushroom mixture.
❺ Toast until the bread edges are brown and the mushroom mixture has heated through. Serve immediately.

Scrambled Egg on Toast

Preparation and cooking time: 3 minutes. Serves 1.

This is a favourite for a cooked breakfast or quick lunch. However be warned, if you don't wash the pan up afterwards you will be very unpopular with your flatmates! The first time it may be tricky to judge when to put the toast on so that the egg and toast are ready together, but after a couple of goes you'll find this easy enough.

2 slices of buttered toast
2 eggs, beaten
1 tablespoon milk

1 tablespoon soft margarine
salt and pepper

❶ If possible, keep the toast warm whilst making the scrambled eggs. Otherwise set it going when the egg is partly cooked.
❷ Beat the egg and milk together. Season.
❸ Melt the margarine in a small saucepan and, when hot, add the egg and milk mixture. Stir whilst cooking over a low heat. Some people like their eggs runny whilst others prefer them firm. I find that it takes 1–2 minutes to reach a medium set.
❹ Serve the scrambled eggs on the buttered toast. Eat it immediately.

Fish Toasties

Preparation and cooking time: 8 minutes. Serves 1.

3 slices of wholemeal bread
120 g (4 oz) can of sardines in tomato sauce

1 teaspoon French mustard
a dash of Worcestershire sauce

❶ Toast the bread on one side.
❷ Meanwhile, mash the other ingredients together.
❸ Cut each bread slice in half and spread the toasted side of 3 halves with fish mixture. Top with the other slices, untoasted-side up.
❹ Grill until brown, and then turn the toasties over and grill the last untoasted side until brown. Serve immediately.

Tuna and Mango Toasts

Preparation and cooking time: 7 minutes. Serves 1.

I occasionally add some mashed banana to this – the flavours blend very well.

2 slices of bread or 1 roll, halved lengthways
99 g can of tuna in brine, drained
1 teaspoon soft margarine

1 tablespoon mango chutney
1 banana (optional)

❶ Toast the bread on one side and then turn it over.
❷ Toast until the bread is starting to crispen but is not yet brown.
❸ Mash the other ingredients together, adding half the banana if you like. Spread over the bread. Top with sliced banana if you like and then toast for 2 minutes. Serve immediately.

Devilled Corned-Beef Toasts

Preparation and cooking time: 10 minutes. Serves 1–2.

4 slices of bread
4 teaspoons soft margarine
1 teaspoon French mustard

2 teaspoons tomato ketchup
3 slices premium corned beef, mashed

❶ Toast the bread on one side.
❷ Mix the margarine, mustard and ketchup together.
❸ Turn the bread over and toast until the bread is starting to crispen, but is not yet brown. Spread with the margarine mixture and top each slice with corned beef.
❹ Toast for two minutes. Serve immediately.

Pizza Toasts

Preparation and cooking time: 7 minutes. Serves 1.

Another lunchtime snack that is very popular as it's so quick to prepare.

2 slices of bread, or 1 muffin, split

1 teaspoon pesto sauce

2 teaspoons tomato purée

25 g (1 oz) cheese, grated

pepper

❶ Heat the grill and toast the bread or muffin on one side, turn it over and toast until the second side crispens, but is not yet brown.

❷ Mix together the pesto and tomato purée and spread them over the bread or muffin. Sprinkle with the cheese and season with pepper.

❸ Grill for 2 minutes, until the cheese bubbles and begins to brown.

Cheese Rarebit

Preparation and cooking time: 7 minutes. Serves 1.

This is another firm student favourite. This was the snack that kept me going when writing essays; and I often succumbed to it after returning late from a night out.

2 slices of bread

50 g (2 oz) cheese, grated

1 teaspoon French mustard

2 teaspoons soft margarine

a dash of Worcestershire sauce

❶ Toast the bread on one side. Turn it over and toast until the bread crispens but is not yet brown.

❷ Meanwhile, mash the cheese, mustard and margarine together. Spread them over the toast and sprinkle with some Worcestershire sauce.

❸ Grill for 2 minutes until bubbling and brown. Serve immediately. Yummy!

French Toast

Preparation and cooking time: 10 minutes. Serves 1.

I often serve this with a banana that I have grilled whole in its skin for 4–5 minutes. It is then easily mashed and can be used as a topping for this toast.

1 egg, beaten

2 tablespoons milk

1 teaspoon sugar

a pinch of ground cinnamon

2 medium-size or 3–4 small slices of bread

a little butter for frying

❶ Mix together the egg, milk, sugar and cinnamon in a shallow bowl.
❷ Soak the bread in the egg mixture (this amount of liquid should be absorbed by two medium-size slices of bread).
❸ Heat a frying-pan and melt the butter.
❹ Fry the bread on both sides until brown.

Variation: another version of this is called cinnamon toast. For this you lightly toast your bread on both sides. Mash together some butter, sugar and cinnamon and spread this on the bread. Then grill until the butter bubbles and the sugar caramelises.

Chilli-Bean Toasts

Preparation time: 5 minutes. Makes 4–6 slices.

As this keeps for a few days in the refrigerator, it can be made ahead and used as a lunchtime snack.

213 g can of red kidney beans, drained

1 tablespoon water

1 tablespoon tomato purée

1–2 teaspoons chilli sauce

salt and pepper

hot buttered toast, to serve

❶ Mash the kidney beans to a paste.
❷ Add the water, tomato purée and chilli sauce to taste. Season well with salt and pepper.

❸ Use as a topping for the toast, or dip the toast into it.

Substantial Soups

What a wonderful invention soup is! No one has to be a cookery genius to whizz up a soup, nor does it have to take hours. A good, honest soup is both quick and easy to make and it is a cheap way of producing a sustaining and nourishing meal.

I think soups are particularly valuable in the student's diet as they are a good way of using both fresh vegetables and items such as beans and lentils: everyone knows these are good for you, but some people have problems fitting them into their cooking.

I love to add 'a little something' to my soups, so I commonly stir in some greek-style yogurt, or a spicy chutney. I often serve them with grated cheese or even nuts, and always with a tasty bread.

DIY Leftovers Soup

Preparation and cooking time: 10 minutes. Serves 1.

It is not often that students have any leftovers, but occasionally, when you have been home for the weekend and been treated to a Sunday roast, you may be able to procure the leftovers to bring back to college. This is the ideal way to use them up.

300 ml (10 fl oz) meat stock
125 g (4 oz) cooked meat, diced

250 g (8 oz) cooked vegetables, diced
salt and pepper

❶ Heat up the meat stock and then add the other ingredients.

❷ Bring to the boil, and then simmer for 2–3 minutes.

❸ Season to taste and serve hot.

Curried-Bean Soup

Preparation and cooking time: 10 minutes. Serves 1.

If I am having this as my main meal of the day, I tend to serve it with yogurt, to which I add some chopped fresh mint and mango chutney. I stir both of these into the soup, and eat it with chapatis or naan bread.

1 tablespoon oil
1 onion, chopped

213 g can of curried beans
150 ml (¼ pint) boiling water

❶ Heat the oil in a saucepan and fry the onion for 5 minutes.
❷ Add the other ingredients and simmer gently for 5 minutes. Stir whilst cooking and mash some of the beans against the side of the pan to thicken the soup. Serve hot.

Tuna and Sweetcorn Soup

Preparation and cooking time: 10 minutes. Serves 1.

This is a thick, luscious soup that is a very popular lunch dish in our house. When I am making enough for two, I double the ingredients, apart from the onion and oil. It's nice with garlic bread.

1 tablespoon oil
1 onion, chopped
99 g can of tuna in brine, drained
230 g can of chopped tomatoes
2 teaspoons tomato purée

2 tablespoons canned sweetcorn
100 ml (3½ fl oz) boiling water
salt and pepper
1 tablespoon greek-style yogurt, to serve

❶ Heat the oil in a saucepan and fry the onion for 5 minutes.
❷ Add the rest of the ingredients, except the yogurt. Season to taste and simmer very gently for 4 minutes.
❸ Before serving, stir in the greek-style yogurt. Do not reheat vigorously or bring to the boil when you have added the yogurt, or the yogurt will curdle.

Vegetable Soup

Preparation time: 20 minutes + 30 minutes cooking. Serves 2.

This is a basic recipe for soup: once you have made it, you can add different seasonings, such as herbs, red pesto, cheese, etc. I sometimes add canned beans or cooked pasta. The choices are endless!

1 kg (2 lb) root vegetables, e.g. onions, carrots, leeks and parsnips, diced

600 ml (1 pint) water
salt and pepper

❶ Put the vegetables and water in a saucepan and bring to the boil.

❷ Cover tightly and simmer for 30 minutes until the vegetables are soft.

❸ Mash some of the vegetables against the side of the pan to thicken the soup. Season well before serving hot.

French Onion Soup

Preparation time: 15 minutes + 20 minutes cooking. Serves 2.

This makes an ideal dish for entertaining a friend. Whilst you are eating this soup and sharing a bottle of red wine, it is easy to evoke an atmosphere of *joie de vivre*! If you can run to it, Gruyère cheese is very good here.

4 tablespoons (about 75 g/3 oz) butter
4 onions, sliced thinly
1 tablespoon plain flour
1 garlic clove, chopped
2 beef stock cubes, dissolved in 900 ml
** (1½ pints) boiling water**

salt and pepper
To serve:
4 slices of french bread, plus extra to serve
50 g (2 oz) cheese, preferably Gruyère, grated

❶ Heat the butter in a saucepan and fry the onions until they are very soft and turning brown at the edges (about 10 minutes). This gives the soup its distinctive flavour.

❷ Stir the flour and garlic into the onion and mix in well. Add the stock and season well.

❸ Bring to the boil and simmer for 20 minutes.

❹ Meanwhile, preheat the grill. Sprinkle the four slices of the bread with the cheese. Grill for 1 minute, until the cheese starts to melt.

❺ Put the soup into bowls, and float two slices of bread on each. Serve immediately, with the extra bread for dipping when you have eaten the cheesy bits.

Spiced Lentil Soup

Preparation time: 10 minutes + 20 minutes cooking. Serves 2.

This is a lovely thick soup that I like to serve with hot naan bread.

1 tablespoon oil
1 onion, chopped finely
1 garlic clove, chopped
2–3 teaspoons mild curry paste

125 g (4 oz) red lentils
397 g can of chopped tomatoes
600 ml (1 pint) hot water
2 tablespoons coconut milk powder

❶ Heat the oil in a saucepan. Fry the onion and garlic for 5 minutes.
❷ Add the curry paste and stir-fry for 1 minute.
❸ Add the lentils, tomatoes and half the water. Simmer uncovered for 10 minutes.

❹ Mix the rest of the water and coconut milk powder together and add to the soup. Cover and simmer for a further 10 minutes. Check that the lentils are cooked. Serve hot.

Spicy Sausage Soup

Preparation and cooking time: 25 minutes. Serves 2.

This is a very spicy soup that I usually serve with thick natural yogurt or soured cream – to take away some of the heat!

1 tablespoon oil
1 onion, chopped
1 leek, sliced thinly
½ savoy cabbage, stem removed, chopped
900 ml (1½ pints) hot water

1 vegetable stock cube
1 tablespoon pesto
1 teaspoon hot pepper sauce
1 spicy snack sausage, chopped

❶ Heat the oil in a saucepan. Fry the onion for 5 minutes. Add the leek and stir-fry for 1 minute.
❷ Add the cabbage and 150 ml (¼ pint) of the water. Cover and cook on a low heat for 5 minutes.

❸ Meanwhile dissolve the stock cube in the remaining water.
❹ Add the rest of the ingredients to the soup, cover and cook for a further 5 minutes. Serve hot.

Quick-Fries

An essential tool for students is the wok or frying-pan, and then nothing is easier to prepare than one of these quick-fry dishes. Very often, even after a hard day's lectures and tutorials, speed is of the essence, because you have essay deadlines to meet. These recipes are the answer: all you need is a sharp knife and your frying-pan and you can be sitting down to your meal in a matter of minutes!

Fruity Teriyaki Lamb

Preparation and cooking time: 20 minutes. Serves 4.

This can also be made using pork chops instead of lamb. Instead of prunes, you could use fresh or canned apricots, sliced apple or clementine segments.

2 tablespoons oil

500 g (1 lb) lamb chump chops, boned and
   sliced thinly

a bunch of spring onions, chopped

150 g jar of teriyaki stir-fry sauce or spicy
   oriental stir-fry sauce

440 g can of prunes, pitted and halved, or
   440 g can of apricots

198 g can of sweetcorn

❶ Heat the oil in a wok or frying-pan and stir-fry the lamb on a high heat for 5–6 minutes, until brown. Turn the heat down.

❷ Add the spring onions and stir-fry for 2 minutes. Add the rest of the ingredients and stir whilst heating through.

❸ Serve immediately. Although this can be used as a topping for baked potatoes, I would normally serve it with egg-noodles or boiled rice.

Sweet and Sour Aubergine

Preparation time: 15 minutes + 10 minutes cooking. Serves 1–2.

3–5 tablespoons oil

1 onion, chopped

2.5 cm (1-inch) piece of fresh root ginger, coarsely chopped or grated

1 aubergine, sliced

1 tablespoon dark brown muscovado sugar

juice of 1 lime

150 ml (¼ pint) boiling water

❶ Heat a tablespoon of the oil in a large frying-pan or saucepan and fry the onion for 5 minutes.

❷ Add the ginger and fry for a further minute.

❸ Add about 2 tablespoons more oil, and the aubergine slices. Fry them for a few minutes on each side until brown. You may need to do this in batches; add more oil as necessary.

❹ Add the sugar, lime juice and water and bring to the boil. Cover and simmer for 10 minutes. Serve with noodles or rice, if you like.

Burgers and Beans

Preparation and cooking time: 15 minutes. Serves 1–2.

I always serve this with instant mashed potato, and, depending how much mash you make up, this recipe will serve either one or two people. It is a popular meal with kid brothers or sisters!

1 tablespoon oil

1 onion, sliced

2 quarter-pounders with onion, each sliced into 4 or 5 strips

205 g can of beans in tomato sauce

❶ Heat the oil in a frying-pan and fry the onion, on a high heat, for 5 minutes.

❷ Push to one side of the pan and place the beefburger strips in the pan. Fry each strip for a minute on each side.

❸ Mix the onion and the beefburger strips together and turn the heat down.

❹ Add the beans and stir whilst heating through. Serve immediately.

lecture 11am
Tuesday

Dissertation for
next week.

Student Union meeting
Thursday 4pm

Thai-style Chicken

Preparation and cooking time: 15 minutes. Serves 1.

This can be easily doubled to serve two. It goes well with noodles or rice or use it as a topping for baked potatoes. On occasion, I have spiced it up with either a hot mango or lime pickle, or alternatively that 'vicious' West-Indian hot pepper sauce.

1 tablespoon oil

125 g (4 oz) boneless, skinless chicken breast, sliced thinly

3 tablespoons sweetcorn

125 g (4 oz) white cabbage, sliced thinly

1 tablespoon mild curry paste

2 tablespoons coconut milk powder

150 ml (¼ pint) boiling water

1 tablespoon crunchy peanut butter

roughly chopped fresh coriander (optional)

❶ Heat the oil in a frying-pan or wok and stir-fry the chicken for 5 minutes.

❷ Add the sweetcorn, cabbage and the curry paste and stir-fry for a further 2 minutes. Mix the coconut milk powder with the boiling water.

❸ Add the coconut milk mixture and peanut butter to the pan. Stir and bring to the boil.

❹ Simmer gently for 2 minutes and sprinkle with the coriander before serving, if you like.

Chinese-style Cabbage

Preparation and cooking time: 15 minutes. Serves 2.

2 tablespoons oil

½ savoy cabbage, stem removed, sliced thinly

4 spring onions, sliced

3 garlic cloves, chopped

2 tablespoons soy sauce

1 tablespoon oyster sauce

a dash of chilli sauce

150 ml (¼ pint) boiling water

2 tablespoons flaked almonds, toasted

1 tablespoon pumpkin seeds

❶ Heat the oil in a large frying-pan or wok and stir-fry the cabbage, spring onions and garlic for 5 minutes.

❷ Stir in the sauces, add the water and bring to the boil. Cover and simmer for 3 minutes.

❸ Just before serving add the almonds and pumpkin seeds, and stir through. Serve immediately.

Black-eyed Bean and Mushroom Bhajee

Preparation and cooking time: 15 minutes. Serves 2.

Although the fresh coriander in this recipe is optional, you should try it at least once, as coriander really adds to the finished dish. Serve with naan bread.

2 tablespoons oil

1 onion, chopped

2 garlic cloves, chopped

250 g (8 oz) button mushrooms, quartered

1 tablespoon mild curry paste

230 g can of chopped tomatoes

432 g can of black-eyed beans, drained

1 tablespoon greek-style yogurt

1 tablespoon chopped fresh coriander

(optional)

❶ Heat the oil in a saucepan and fry the onion and garlic for 5 minutes.

❷ Add the mushrooms and stir-fry for 2 minutes.

❸ Add the curry paste and stir it through. Add the chopped tomatoes and the beans. Simmer gently for 3 minutes.

❹ Stir in the yogurt and the coriander (if using) and serve immediately. Do not reheat once you have added the yogurt.

Pork and Banana Korma

Preparation and cooking time: 20 minutes. Serves 1.

This is a quick and tasty version of a much-loved curry dish that is served in many Indian restaurants. It can easily serve two if you double the amount of pork, banana, curry paste and cream used.

1 tablespoon oil

1 onion, chopped finely

1 garlic clove, chopped finely

1 green pepper, de-seeded and chopped

175 g (6 oz) boneless pork shoulder steaks,
    cubed

1 tablespoon mild curry paste

2.5 cm (1-inch) piece of fresh root ginger,
    coarsely chopped or grated

2 tablespoons single cream

1 banana, sliced

1 tablespoon flaked almonds, toasted

❶ Heat the oil in a saucepan and fry the onion, garlic and pepper for 5 minutes.

❷ Add the pork and fry for a further 5 minutes.

❸ Now add the curry paste and ginger and stir through.

❹ Add the cream and banana and heat through.

❺ Stir in the flaked almonds just before serving, so that they retain their crispness. Serve with rice.

Tuna Hash

Preparation and cooking time: 15 minutes. Serves 1–2.

Another useful standby for when you are busy and want something that is quick and easy to make. It serves one person with a healthy appetite, or can be shared between two if served with baked beans.

1 tablespoon oil
1 small onion, chopped finely
1 garlic clove, chopped
½ red pepper, de-seeded and chopped finely
198 g can of tuna, drained

a dash of Worcestershire sauce
a serving of instant mashed potato made up
   with 150 ml (5 fl oz) water
salt and pepper

❶ Heat the oil in a frying-pan and fry the onion, garlic and pepper for 5 minutes.
❷ Stir in the rest of the ingredients, seasoning well. Flatten down into a potato cake and cook for 2 minutes without stirring.

❸ Now stir up the mixture so that the brown bits from the underside are mixed in.
❹ Flatten the mixture again and cook for a further 2 minutes. Serve immediately. (I adore this with tomato ketchup!)

Spinach and Chick-pea Bhajee

Preparation and cooking time: 5 minutes. Serves 2.

A very quick, curry-flavoured stir-fry dish that takes only minutes to prepare. You can make it with fresh spinach if you have some (it's cheap from April to July), in which case you should use about 250 g (8 oz) spinach per person.

2 tablespoons oil
4 spring onions, sliced
1 garlic clove, chopped
420 g can of chick-peas, drained
270 g can of English leaf spinach, drained

2 tablespoons tomato purée
1 tablespoon mild curry paste
2 tablespoons chopped fresh coriander
   (optional)

❶ Heat the oil in a frying-pan and fry the spring onions and garlic for 2 minutes.
❷ Add the rest of the ingredients and stir-fry until they are hot, about 2–3

minutes. Make sure you break up the spinach, as it tends to cling together. Serve immediately; it's nice with poppadums.

Pasta Dishes

There is an ever-increasing variety of pasta on the market in innumerable shapes, sizes and colours. Pasta's virtues are many; it's cheap to buy, easy to store and cook, and incredibly versatile. Once you have worked your way through the recipes here, why not have a go at making up your own? Pasta goes well with many vegetables, as well as cheeses and nutty sauces. The only thing limiting the number of dishes you can make with pasta is your imagination!

Mushroom and Garlic Tagliatelle

Preparation and cooking time: 15 minutes. Serves 2.

200 g (7 oz) egg and spinach tagliatelle
1 tablespoon oil
1 leek, sliced thinly
125 g (4 oz) mushrooms, halved

100 g tub of soft cheese with garlic and herbs
4 tablespoons milk
black pepper

❶ Cook the tagliatelle in plenty of lightly salted boiling water according to the pack instructions.

❷ Meanwhile, heat the oil and fry the leek and mushrooms over a high heat until soft and brown, about 5 minutes.

Turn down the heat and add the soft cheese and milk. Melt down into a sauce and heat through, stirring frequently.

❸ Drain the tagliatelle and toss with the sauce. Season with black pepper and serve immediately.

Pasta with Butter-beans and Pesto Sauce

Preparation and cooking time: 15 minutes. Serves 1.

This is a very versatile recipe. Instead of the beans you could use cooked peas or sweetcorn; and at times, I have replaced the beans with tuna or cooked meat, such as ham or chicken.

75 g (3 oz) pasta, e.g. tagliatelle
1 tablespoon tomato purée
1–2 tablespoons pesto sauce

1 tablespoon olive oil or soft margarine
220 g can of butter-beans, drained
salt and pepper

❶ Cook the pasta in plenty of lightly salted boiling water according to the pack instructions.

❷ Meanwhile, mix the other ingredients together in a bowl and season them with salt and pepper.

❸ Drain the pasta and return it to the pan. Add the other ingredients, mix well, and heat through gently before serving. Stir to prevent the pasta sticking to the pan.

Pasta with Peanutty Pork

Preparation and cooking time: 20 minutes. Serves 2.

I have made this dish substituting tagliatelle for the pasta bows. The peanut sauce can also be made without the pasta and used as a topping for baked potatoes.

125 g (4 oz) farfalle (pasta bows)
1 tablespoon oil
1 small yellow pepper, sliced
375 g (12 oz) boneless pork shoulder steaks, trimmed of fat and cubed

4 spring onions, chopped
2 tablespoons crunchy peanut butter
6 tablespoons milk
salt and pepper

❶ Cook the pasta bows in plenty of lightly salted boiling water according to the pack instructions.
❷ Meanwhile, heat the oil in a saucepan and fry the pepper and pork for 5–6 minutes until they begin to brown.

❸ Stir in the spring onions and fry for a further 2 minutes.
❹ Add the peanut butter and milk and melt down into a sauce, stirring frequently. Heat through.
❺ Drain the pasta and serve with the peanut sauce poured over on the plate.

Cheesy Bows

Preparation and cooking time: 15 minutes. Serves 1.

This is very rich and calorific, but also delicious! It's nice served with broccoli.

75 g (3 oz) farfalle (pasta bows)
1 tablespoon olive oil or soft margarine
1 small onion, chopped
2 × 16 g soft cheese with garlic and herbs (from the pick-'n'-mix section)

3 tablespoons milk
50 g (2 oz) cheese, grated
salt and pepper

❶ Cook the pasta in plenty of lightly salted boiling water, according to the pack instructions.
❷ Meanwhile, heat the oil or margarine in a frying-pan and fry the onion for 5 minutes.
❸ Mix in the soft cheese, add the milk

and melt down into a sauce, stirring frequently.
❹ Drain the pasta and return it to the pan. Immediately add the sauce and the grated cheese and toss well together. Season with salt and pepper and serve immediately.

Tomato and Cannellini Beans with Pasta

Preparation and cooking time:

125 g (4 oz) pasta, e.g. spirali (spirals)
1 tablespoon oil
1 onion, chopped
2 garlic cloves, chopped

250 g (8 oz) creamed tomatoes
1 tablespoon red pesto
420 g can of cannellini beans, drained
grated cheese, to serve (optional)

❶ Cook the pasta in plenty of lightly salted boiling water according to the pack instructions.
❷ Meanwhile, heat the oil in another saucepan and fry the onion and garlic for 5 minutes.
❸ Add the creamed tomatoes and red pesto, and simmer until you have a thick sauce, approximately 3 minutes.
❹ Add the cannellini beans and stir whilst heating through for 3–4 minutes.
❺ When the pasta is cooked, drain it and serve the sauce poured over the pasta on the plate. Serve with grated cheese, if you like.

Pasta with Creamed Tuna Sauce

Preparation and cooking time: 15 minutes. Serves 2.

15 minutes. Serves 2.

175 g (6 oz) pasta, e.g. fusilli (twists)
1 tablespoon oil
1 onion, chopped finely

198 g can of tuna in brine, drained
142 ml (5 fl oz) carton of single cream
salt and pepper

❶ Cook the pasta in plenty of lightly salted boiling water according to the pack instructions.
❷ Meanwhile, heat the oil in another saucepan and fry the onion until it is soft and starting to colour, 5–6 minutes.
❸ Add the tuna and cream and stir whilst heating through. Season to taste with salt and pepper.
❹ Drain the pasta and toss it with the sauce.

Simple Spaghetti Sauce

Preparation and cooking time: 15 minutes. Serves 1.

If you have some sharp scissors, I always find that it is easier to cut up anchovies than to chop them. To stretch this recipe to serve two, just add some chopped tomatoes with the tomato purée and pesto, and double the amount of spaghetti.

50–75 g (2–3 oz) spaghetti

1 tablespoon (about 1 oz (30 g)) butter

1 garlic clove, crushed

50 g can of anchovies in olive oil, plus the oil from the can

1 tablespoon tomato purée

1 tablespoon red pesto

chilli or hot pepper sauce (optional)

❶ Cook the spaghetti in plenty of lightly salted boiling water according to the pack instructions.

❷ Meanwhile, in another saucepan, melt the butter and cook the garlic, anchovies and the oil from the can over a very low heat for 5 minutes, or until the anchovies melt into a sauce. Stir frequently.

❸ Add the other ingredients, including the chilli or hot pepper sauce if you like it, and continue to cook until the spaghetti is ready.

❹ Drain the spaghetti and return it to the pan. Immediately toss it with the sauce and serve at once.

Chilli-pork Noodles

Preparation and cooking time: 15 minutes. Serves 2.

1 'layer' of egg-noodles

1 tablespoon oil

1 green pepper, de-seeded and chopped finely

250 g (8 oz) boneless pork shoulder steaks, cubed

230 g can of chopped tomatoes

1 tablespoon chilli sauce

1 tablespoon tomato purée

1 tablespoon soy sauce

❶ Put the noodles in a large bowl and cover them with boiling water. Leave to soak, according to the pack instructions.

❷ Meanwhile, heat the oil in a saucepan and fry the pepper and pork together for 5 minutes.

❸ Add the rest of the ingredients and cook, stirring, for a further 2 minutes.

❹ When the noodles are ready, drain them and add them to the saucepan. Mix together thoroughly and serve at once.

Noodles with Chinese-style Lamb

Preparation and cooking time: 15 minutes. Serves 2.

1 'layer' of egg-noodles

1 tablespoon oil

4 spring onions, sliced thinly

1 red pepper, sliced thinly

175 g (6 oz) boneless lamb leg slices, cubed

198 g can of sweetcorn

1 tablespoon soy sauce

2 tablespoons hoisin sauce

1 teaspoon mint sauce

❶ Put the noodles in a large bowl and cover them with boiling water. Leave them to soak according to the pack instructions.

❷ Meanwhile, heat the oil in a saucepan or frying-pan and fry the spring onions, red pepper and lamb for 5 minutes.

❸ Add the rest of the ingredients and continue to stir-fry for a further minute.

❹ When the noodles are cooked, drain them and add them to the saucepan. Mix together thoroughly and serve at once.

Pasta with Easy Bolognese Sauce

Preparation and cooking time: 15 minutes. Serves 2.

Although nothing like the original Italian *ragù* or bolognese sauce, this is extremely quick, and a popular dish with students. There is no need to serve it with spaghetti: in fact it is much easier to eat with farfalle or fusilli (pasta bows or twists).

For a special occasion, you could use red wine instead of water and simmer the sauce for longer to tenderise the meat. Add fresh basil and sun-dried tomatoes, instead of the red pesto, serving it of course with plenty of red wine!

175 g (6 oz) farfalle or fusilli (pasta bows or
 twists)
1 tablespoon oil
1 onion, chopped finely
1 garlic clove, chopped finely

250 g (8 oz) minced beef
50 g (2 oz) mushrooms, chopped
2 tablespoons tomato purée
1 tablespoon red pesto
salt and pepper

❶ Cook the pasta in plenty of lightly salted boiling water according to the pack instructions.

❷ Meanwhile, heat the oil in another saucepan and fry the onion and garlic until soft, about 5 minutes.

❸ Add the minced beef and stir-fry on the highest heat for 2 minutes, until browned.

❹ Add the mushrooms and stir-fry for 1 minute.

❺ Lower the heat, add the tomato purée and the red pesto, and season well with salt and pepper.

❻ Now add just a little water to make a sauce and simmer until the pasta has cooked.

❼ Drain the pasta and serve it topped with the sauce.

Rice and Grain Dishes

Rice is a cheap, nourishing and versatile standby. Rice and grain dishes are popular throughout the world. They are extremely useful because any leftovers can quickly be transformed into a rice salad for the following lunchtime. This applies not only to rice but to couscous and bulgar wheat as well. If you have not tried these grains before, I urge you to experiment with them – they are even easier to cook than rice.

For the risotto dishes, I have used long-grain rice, not the traditional 'Arborio' risotto rice, so you don't have to stock up on different kinds of rice. But do try risotto rice if you prefer.

Chick-pea Pilaff

Preparation and cooking time: 30 minutes. Serves 1.

50 g (2 oz) bulgar wheat

2 tablespoons oil

75 g (3 oz) broccoli, chopped

50 g (2 oz) mushrooms, chopped

2 tablespoons canned sweetcorn

½ x 420 g can of chick-peas, drained

1 onion, sliced

2 garlic cloves, chopped

1 tablespoon mild curry paste

2 tablespoons coconut milk powder, dissolved in 150 ml (¼ pint) boiling water

❶ Put the bulgar wheat in a bowl and cover it with boiling water.

❷ Meanwhile, heat half the oil in a saucepan and stir-fry the broccoli and mushrooms for 3 minutes. Add the sweetcorn and chick-peas. Mix well and set aside.

❸ In a frying-pan, heat the remaining oil and fry the onion and garlic for 10 minutes.

❹ Add the curry paste and stir through. Add the coconut milk to the frying-pan. Simmer for 3 minutes.

❺ Meanwhile, drain the bulgar wheat and add it to the saucepan of broccoli, etc. Mix well and gently heat it through. Mix in the curried onion sauce and serve at once.

Lamb with Couscous

Preparation and cooking time: 10 minutes. Serves 1.

40 g (1½ oz) couscous

1 tablespoon oil

1 lamb chop, boned and cubed

1 small onion, chopped finely

2 tablespoons hoisin sauce

3 tablespoons water

❶ Cook the couscous as directed on the pack. This makes a decent-size serving of 100 g (3½ oz) cooked couscous.

❷ Meanwhile, heat the oil in a frying-pan and fry the lamb and onion until brown, approximately 5 minutes.

❸ Stir in the hoisin sauce and water and stir-fry for 1 minute. Serve with the cooked couscous. Courgettes are a good accompaniment to this.

Tuna and Sweetcorn Risotto

Preparation time: 10 minutes + 15 minutes cooking. Serves 2.

1 tablespoon oil

1 onion, chopped

1 red pepper, de-seeded and chopped

175 g (6 oz) American long-grain rice

1 vegetable stock cube, dissolved in 450 ml (15 fl oz) boiling water

185 g can of tuna in brine, drained

198 g can of sweetcorn, drained

❶ Heat the oil in a frying-pan and fry the onion and pepper for 5 minutes.

❷ Add the rice and stir it through. Now add the stock and bring it to the boil. Turn the heat down and let it simmer for 10–15 minutes, until the stock has been absorbed.

❸ Add the tuna and sweetcorn and stir them in. Heat them through and then serve at once.

Vegetable Biryani

Preparation and cooking time: 20 minutes. Serves 2.

This is a quick and very tasty vegetarian biryani. I sometimes stir some cooked green lentils into the rice mixture, and serve poppadums and naan bread with it.

2 tablespoons oil

2 tablespoons mild curry paste

175 g (6 oz) American long-grain rice

175 g (6 oz) okra, chopped

1 small cauliflower, chopped coarsely

1 vegetable stock cube, dissolved in 600 ml (1 pint) boiling water

1 onion, chopped

2 garlic cloves, chopped finely

4 tablespoons coconut milk powder, dissolved in 300 ml (½ pint) boiling water

❶ Heat 1 tablespoon of the oil and 1 tablespoon of the curry paste in a large frying-pan, and stir in the rice.

❷ Add the okra, cauliflower and stock. Bring to the boil, cover and simmer for 10–15 minutes, until the vegetables and rice are cooked.

❸ Meanwhile, heat the remaining oil in a small saucepan and fry the onion and garlic for 10 minutes.

❹ Add the rest of the curry paste and the coconut milk. Simmer gently for 2 minutes.

❺ Drain the vegetable mixture and serve it with the coconut sauce poured over on the plate.

Minced Meat Pilaff

Preparation time: 20 minutes + 15 minutes cooking. Serves 2.

Another popular favourite in our house. In this recipe I have used minced beef, but it works equally well with minced lamb.

1 tablespoon oil

1 onion, chopped finely

2 garlic cloves, chopped finely

250 g (8 oz) minced beef

125 g (4 oz) bulgar wheat

600 ml (1 pint) boiling water

125 g (4 oz) peas

25 g (1 oz) raisins

2 tablespoons greek-style yogurt

1 teaspoon mint sauce

salt and pepper

❶ Heat the oil in a large frying-pan and fry the onion and garlic for 5 minutes.

❷ Add the minced beef and cook for a further 5 minutes.

❸ Now add the bulgar wheat and stir through, before adding the boiling water, peas and raisins. Season well with salt and pepper.

❹ Bring to the boil, and then simmer for 15 minutes, or until the water is absorbed.

❺ Stir together the yogurt and mint sauce, and serve with the pilaff.

Spicy Sausage and Couscous

Preparation and cooking time: 12 minutes. Serves 1.

40 g (1½ oz) couscous

1 tablespoon oil

1 small onion, chopped

1 garlic clove, chopped

1 spicy snack sausage, sliced

125 g (4 oz) peas

230 g can of chopped tomatoes

1 tablespoon tomato purée

2 tablespoons water

2 teaspoons chilli sauce

❶ Make up the couscous as directed on the pack. This amount makes a 100 g (3½ oz) serving of cooked couscous.

❷ Heat the oil in a saucepan and fry the onion and garlic for 5 minutes.

❸ Add the rest of the ingredients, and simmer for 2–3 minutes.

❹ Serve with the couscous.

Mushroom and Cashew-nut Risotto

Preparation time: 10 minutes + 15 minutes cooking. Serves 2.

2 tablespoons oil

1 onion, chopped

250 g (8 oz) mushrooms, quartered

175 g (6 oz) American long-grain rice

1 vegetable stock cube dissolved in
    450 ml (¾ pint) boiling water

50 g (2 oz) unsalted cashew nuts

❶ Heat the oil in a frying-pan and fry the onion for 2 minutes. Add the mushrooms and stir-fry for a further 3 minutes.

❷ Add the rice and stir through.

❸ Add the vegetable stock and bring to the boil. Cover and simmer for 12–15 minutes, or until the stock is absorbed.

❹ Just before serving, stir through the cashew nuts. Peas or green beans go well with this.

Pork and Peanut Pilaff

Preparation and cooking time: 20 minutes. Serves 1.

50 g (2 oz) bulgar wheat

1 tablespoon oil

1 onion, chopped

1 pork chop, boned and finely diced, or 1
   boneless, skinless chicken breast, diced

1 tablespoon crunchy peanut butter

2 tablespoons coconut milk powder, made up
   with 150 ml (¼ pint) boiling water

❶ Make up the bulgar wheat as directed on the pack.

❷ Heat the oil in a frying-pan and fry the onion for 5 minutes.

❸ Add the pork or chicken and fry for a further 5 minutes.

❹ Add the peanut butter and stir through. Add the coconut milk to the frying-pan. Let the mixture simmer gently for 3 minutes.

❺ Serve with the bulgar wheat. Carrots make a good accompaniment.

One-Pot Dishes

These are my all-time-favourite dishes: I guess it is because I am so lazy! I love the idea of putting everything in a pot and then only having to come back at a later stage to an inviting smell and an enjoyable meal. Obviously, these dishes do take some time to cook – but the result is well worth the wait.

Mexican Pork and Vegetable Casserole

Preparation time: 5 minutes + 2 hours cooking. Serves 4.

This is one of our all-time-favourite casseroles. It may take a while to cook, but the preparation couldn't be simpler, as it uses a pack of ready-prepared and chopped casserole vegetables.

397 g can of chopped tomatoes

432 g can of red kidney beans in chilli sauce

2 teaspoons French mustard

375 g (12 oz) pack of fresh casserole vegetables

500 g (1 lb) boneless pork shoulder steaks, diced

142 ml (5 fl oz) carton of soured cream

a packet of tortilla chips

150 g (5 oz) mozzarella cheese, grated

❶ Preheat the oven to Gas Mark 4/ 180°C/350°F.

❷ Mix the tomatoes, beans, mustard, vegetables and pork in a casserole dish. Cover and cook for 1¾ hours.

❸ Spoon the soured cream over the casserole and top with enough tortilla chips to cover the surface (the rest of the chips can be eaten alongside the casserole). Sprinkle with cheese and cook, uncovered, for 15 minutes.

Mediterranean Lamb Casserole

Preparation time: 25 minutes + 1¼ hours cooking. Serves 4.

This is a very popular casserole in our house – particularly when served with lashings of garlic bread.

1 aubergine, sliced

about 4 tablespoons oil

1 onion, chopped

2 garlic cloves, chopped

1 green pepper, de-seeded and chopped

1 courgette, sliced

500 g (1 lb) boneless lamb neck fillet, cubed

397 g can of chopped tomatoes

1 tablespoon red pesto

1 tablespoon tomato purée

420 g can of chick-peas, drained

❶ Preheat the oven to Gas Mark 4/ 180°C/350°F, and set the grill to heat up.

❷ Put the aubergine slices on the rack of a grill pan and brush with about a tablespoon of oil. Cook under the grill until brown and then turn and repeat with the other side. This takes 3–4 minutes.

❸ Meanwhile, heat the remaining 3 tablespoons of oil in a frying-pan and fry the onion, garlic and pepper for 5 minutes. Add the courgette and fry for 2 minutes. Remove to a casserole dish.

❹ Fry the lamb until brown and then stir into the casserole dish, with all of the other ingredients.

❺ Top with the aubergine slices, cover and cook in the preheated oven for 1¼ hours.

French Chicken in a Pot

Preparation time: 25 minutes + 1½ hours cooking. Serves 4.

This is a favourite for Sunday lunch with friends. The only preparation is in the chopping up of the vegetables. Then you can start that overdue essay or inscrutable maths problem whilst you wait for your delicious dinner.

1 leek, sliced

2 turnips, sliced thinly

2 carrots, cut into matchsticks

2 parsnips, cut into 8

1 swede, diced

1.1 kg (2½ lb) corn-fed chicken

50 g (2 oz) softened butter

a good pinch of freeze-dried tarragon

1 chicken stock cube dissolved in
  300 ml (½ pint) boiling water

8 garlic cloves, unpeeled

2 tablespoons oil

375 g (12 oz) potato, cut in wedges

salt and pepper

❶ Preheat the oven to Gas Mark 5/ 190°C/375°F.

❷ Put the vegetables into a large casserole dish, and place the chicken on top.

❸ Mix the butter with the tarragon and place half of the mixture in the chicken cavity. Dot the rest of the butter mixture over the chicken and vegetables.

❹ Pour the stock over the chicken and vegetables, and season with salt and pepper.

❺ Put the garlic cloves amongst the vegetables.

❻ Cover and cook for one hour.

❼ Turn the oven up to Gas Mark 7/ 220°C/425°F, uncover, and continue to cook.

❽ Meanwhile, heat the oil in a frying-pan until hot and stir-fry the potato until brown (about 8 minutes).

❾ Place the browned potato on top of the casserole and continue to cook for 15 minutes.

❿ When serving, make sure that everyone gets some chicken breast as well as either a wing or leg. (The meat is very tender and can easily be divided up.)

Lasagne

Preparation time: 25 minutes + 45 minutes cooking. Serves 4.

There can't be many students who at some point in their culinary career don't attempt to make lasagne. This is absolutely the easiest recipe for lasagne that you could try. The making of the béchamel or cheese sauce is usually the biggest stumbling block for novices, so here I have used a sauce that you can buy.

1 tablespoon oil
1 onion, chopped
2 garlic cloves, chopped
500 g (1 lb) minced beef
1 tablespoon tomato purée
397 g can of chopped tomatoes with basil

125 g (4 oz) no-precooking-required lasagne
  sheets
400 g (13 oz) carton of salsa lasagne sauce
50 g (2 oz) cheese, grated
salt and pepper

❶ Preheat the oven to Gas Mark 6/ 200°C/400°F.

❷ Heat the oil in a saucepan and fry the onion and garlic for 5 minutes.

❸ Add the minced beef and continue to fry for a further 5 minutes, stirring frequently, until the meat is browned.

❹ Add the tomato purée and chopped tomatoes, season and simmer for 10 minutes.

❺ Layer half of the meat mixture into a lasagne dish, cover with half of the lasagne sheets and half of the salsa lasagne sauce. Continue with the rest of the meat mixture, lasagne and sauce.

❻ Sprinkle with the cheese and bake in the preheated oven for 45 minutes.

Mushroom and Lentil Lasagne
Preparation time: 25 minutes + 45 minutes cooking. Serves 4.

This is a vegetarian version of lasagne. You can substitute a carton of ready-made salsa lasagne sauce for the cheese sauce in this recipe, if you don't feel up to attempting the cheese sauce.

2 tablespoons oil

1 onion, chopped

2 garlic cloves, chopped

250 g (8 oz) mushrooms, chopped finely

2 tablespoons tomato purée

1 tablespoon red pesto

397 g can of chopped tomatoes

432 g can of green lentils, drained

125 g (4 oz) no-precooking-required lasagne sheets

50 g (2 oz) cheese, grated

For the cheese sauce:

1 tablespoon soft margarine

1 tablespoon plain wholemeal flour

300 ml (½ pint) milk

a pinch of dry mustard

125 g (4 oz) vegetarian hard cheese, grated

salt and pepper

❶ Preheat the oven to Gas Mark 6/ 200°C/400°F.

❷ Heat 1 tablespoon of oil in a saucepan and fry the onion and garlic for 5 minutes.

❸ Add the rest of the oil and the mushrooms and fry for a further 5 minutes.

❹ Add the tomato purée, red pesto, chopped tomatoes and lentils. Simmer for 5 minutes.

❺ Meanwhile make the cheese sauce: first melt the margarine in a small saucepan. Remove from the heat and mix in the flour and a little of the milk. Return to the heat and slowly add the rest of the milk while stirring. Season with dry mustard and salt and pepper. Cook the sauce over a gentle heat for a minute, and then add half the cheese.

❻ Put a layer of the mushroom mixture into a lasagne dish, then cover with half of the lasagne sheets and half of the sauce. Continue with the rest of the mushroom mixture, lasagne and sauce.

❼ Sprinkle with the remaining cheese and bake in the preheated oven for 45 minutes.

Sausage Hot-pot

Preparation time: 20 minutes + 2 hours cooking. Serves 4.

This is a good dish for Saturday night or Sunday lunch. It goes down well with some garlic bread and a bottle of red wine.

1 tablespoon oil

454 g (1 lb) Lincolnshire sausages

2 large potatoes, sliced thinly

2 carrots, sliced

1 onion, sliced

250 g (8 oz) mushrooms, sliced

397 g can of chopped tomatoes

1 tablespoon tomato purée

a dash of Worcestershire sauce

1 beef stock cube dissolved in 450 ml (¾ pint) boiling water

25 g (1 oz) butter

salt and pepper

❶ Preheat the oven to Gas Mark 4/ 180°C/350°F.

❷ Heat the oil in a frying-pan and brown the sausages all over, about 10 minutes.

❸ Layer half of the potatoes, and the rest of the vegetables, in a large casserole dish. Stir in the tomatoes and tomato purée. Season well.

❹ Place the sausages on top of the vegetables. Mix the Worcestershire sauce with the stock and pour the stock into the casserole dish.

❺ Top with the rest of the potatoes and dot with the butter.

❻ Cover and cook in the preheated oven for 1¼ hours.

❼ Remove the lid and continue to cook for a further 45 minutes, to brown the potatoes.

Beef Pot-roast

Preparation time: 15 minutes + 3 hours cooking. Serves 4.

This is a favourite for Sunday lunch, since, after the initial preparation, you can quite easily go away and leave it until it is ready. We have eaten it after $2^1/_2$ hours, but prefer it after 3 hours; the vegetables may be well done, but the taste is superb. I usually serve this with mustard or creamed horseradish.

1 tablespoon oil
1.1 kg (2½ lb) boned and rolled brisket of beef
1 potato, sliced
2 turnips, sliced
2 carrots, sliced
1 swede, sliced
1 onion, sliced thinly

1 beef stock cube, dissolved in 300 ml
   (½ pint) boiling water
a pinch of dry mustard
1 garlic clove, crushed
2 teaspoons cornflour (optional)
salt and pepper

❶ Preheat the oven to Gas Mark 3/ 160°C/325°F.
❷ Heat the oil in a large casserole dish and fry the beef until brown on all sides.
❸ Put the vegetables in the bottom of a large, preferably flameproof, casserole dish.
❹ Mix the stock with mustard and garlic. Season well with salt and pepper.
❺ Place the beef on the vegetables and pour the stock over the vegetables.
❻ Cover tightly and cook in the

preheated oven for 3 hours.
❼ To serve, remove the meat and cut it into thick slices (the meat is very tender).
❽ If you wish to thicken the gravy, mix the cornflour with a little cold water, and, whilst the meat is being sliced, add the cornflour mixture to the gravy and vegetables, and stir it in whilst heating gently. (If the casserole dish is not flameproof, pour the gravy into another saucepan, before doing this.) Season and serve with the beef and vegetables.

Veggie Bake

Preparation time: 18 minutes + 1 hour cooking. Serves 4.

A very popular bake to serve to vegetarian friends. In our house, it is always served with garlic bread.

250 g (8 oz) pasta, e.g. farfalle (bows)

2 tablespoons oil

1 onion, chopped

2 garlic cloves, chopped

1 red pepper, de-seeded and chopped

250 g (8 oz) creamed tomatoes

397 g can of chopped tomatoes

1 tablespoon red pesto

125 g (4 oz) broccoli florets, chopped

1 aubergine, sliced

1 large courgette, sliced

150 g (5 oz) mozzarella cheese, grated

salt and pepper

❶ Preheat the oven to Gas Mark 4/ 180°C/350°F.

❷ Cook the pasta for half the time stated on the pack. Drain.

❸ Meanwhile, heat the oil in a saucepan and fry the onion, garlic and pepper for 5 minutes.

❹ Add the creamed tomatoes, chopped tomatoes and red pesto. Season well.

Simmer for 2 minutes to make a thick tomato sauce.

❺ Put the pasta in a greased lasagne dish, cover with the broccoli, aubergine and courgette and sprinkle with the cheese. Spoon the tomato sauce over the bake.

❻ Cook in the preheated oven for 1 hour.

Bean Casserole

Preparation time: 5 minutes + 1 hour cooking. Serves: 2.

Because of the garlic butter, this is not recommended as the ideal supper before a night out!

447 g can of mixed beans in mild chilli sauce

230 g can of chopped tomatoes

1 leek, halved and sliced thinly

1 courgette, halved and sliced thinly

1 tablespoon black treacle

150 ml (¼ pint) boiling water

50 g (2 oz) garlic butter, plus extra to serve

❶ Preheat the oven to Gas Mark 3/ 160°C/325°F.

❷ Mix all the ingredients together in a casserole dish. Cover and cook for 1 hour.

❸ Since we are garlic fanatics, we always serve this in bowls with extra garlic butter stirred into each portion, and with garlic bread!

Puddings and Cakes

Although puddings and cakes are not something to be indulged in every day, we all like to treat ourselves occasionally. The selection I have given here are the ones that I know to be particularly popular with students, with an addition I have recently concocted: Banana and Carrot Cake (page 76). Carrot cake has been a student favourite for years, but I think that this new recipe of mine will be even more popular!

Chocolate Cake

**Preparation time: 25 minutes + 25 minutes cooking + cooling.
Serves 6–8.**

For the cake:
125 g (4 oz) soft margarine
125 g (4 oz) dark-brown soft sugar
2 eggs, beaten
1 tablespoon cocoa powder made up to 125 g
   (4 oz) with self-raising flour

To decorate:
3 × 65 g (2½ oz) Mars bars
25 g (1 oz) butter
50 g (2 oz) dark-brown soft sugar

❶ Preheat the oven to Gas Mark 5/ 190°C/375°F.

❷ Grease an 18 cm (7-inch) cake tin.

❸ Beat together the cake ingredients and spoon into the cake tin. Level the surface by tapping it.

❹ Bake in the preheated oven for 25–30 minutes, until well-risen and brown.

❺ When the cake is cooked, leave it to cool before decorating.

❻ Chop two Mars bars and slice the third. In a heatproof bowl placed over simmering water, melt the chopped Mars bars and butter. Do not let the water touch the underside of the bowl or the chocolate will be spoiled.

❼ When melted (about 10 minutes), beat in the sugar. Spread this icing over the cake. Leave to harden in the refrigerator. Decorate with the Mars bar slices.

Fruit in Crispy Layers

Preparation and cooking time: 15 minutes. Serves 2.

I have used an apple purée in this recipe, but you could substitute other fruit, such as mashed banana, fresh raspberries or blackberries, or other stewed fruits such as plums or rhubarb. If you have the finance, it is nice served with whipped cream.

500 g (1 lb) Bramley apples, diced
1 tablespoon + 25 g (1 oz) soft margarine or
    butter
honey or sugar to taste

75 g (3 oz) fresh wholemeal breadcrumbs
    (approximately 2–3 slices)
25 g (1 oz) dark-brown soft sugar

❶ Cook the apples with the tablespoon of margarine or butter until very soft (about 6–7 minutes). Mash them into a purée, and sweeten to taste with honey or sugar. Leave to cool.

❷ Meanwhile, heat the remaining butter or margarine in a frying-pan and fry the breadcrumbs and sugar until brown and starting to crisp. Leave to cool.

❸ When both are cool, layer the purée and breadcrumbs into two small bowls, finishing with a layer of breadcrumbs.

Apple and Rhubarb Crumble

Preparation time: 25 minutes + 30 minutes cooking. Serves 4–6.

This is the traditional recipe. I sometimes add porridge oats or flaked nuts to the topping. Try it this way first, and then adjust it to your own taste.

1 tablespoon soft margarine or butter
500 g (I lb) Bramley apples, peeled, cored and
    cut into chunks
500 g (1 lb) rhubarb, cut into 2.5 cm (1-inch)
    chunks

2 tablespoons caster sugar
For the crumble topping:
125 g (4 oz) self-raising flour
125 g (4 oz) caster sugar
125 g (4 oz) butter, chopped

❶ Preheat the oven to Gas Mark 6/ 200°C/400°F.

❷ Heat the butter or soft margarine in a saucepan and cook the apples until soft but not falling apart, about 5–6 minutes.

❸ Mix the apples, rhubarb and 2 tablespoons of caster sugar together in a pie dish.

❹ Mix together the flour, sugar and butter for the topping. Keep rubbing the mixture between your fingers until it resembles breadcrumbs.

❺ Completely cover the fruit with the crumble topping.

❻ Bake in the preheated oven for 30 minutes, or until brown.

Flapjacks

Preparation time: 10 minutes + 20 minutes cooking + cooling. Makes 12.

Flapjacks are a student favourite. They are easy to make and disappear quickly!

125 g (4 oz) dark-brown soft sugar
125 g (4 oz) soft margarine

1 tablespoon golden syrup
175 g (6 oz) porridge oats

❶ Preheat the oven to Gas Mark 5/ 190°C/375°F.

❷ Melt the sugar, margarine and syrup together.

❸ Stir in the porridge oats.

❹ Grease an 18 × 28 cm (7 × 11-inch) tin and spoon the mixture into this. Press the mixture down into the tin. Bake in the preheated oven for 20 minutes.

❺ When cooked, leave in the tin but mark into 12 portions and leave to cool. When cold, the flapjacks should have crisped up, so you can remove them from the tin.

Banana and Carrot Cake

Preparation time: 15 minutes + 55 minutes cooking. Serves 9.

In the past I have always been very fond of both banana and carrot cakes: now I have developed a recipe to combine them! Carrot cake has been a student favourite for years, but I think this recipe of mine will be even more popular. You can serve this buttered.

125 g (4 oz) self-raising flour
75 g (3 oz) ground rice
125 g (4 oz) caster sugar
125 g (4 oz) soft margarine
2 eggs, beaten

4 tablespoons milk
a pinch of ground nutmeg
1 pinch of ground cinnamon
1 banana, chopped finely
250 g (8 oz) carrots, grated

❶ Preheat the oven to Gas Mark 4/ 180°C/350°F.

❷ Beat together the flour, ground rice, sugar, margarine, eggs and milk.

❸ Stir in the rest of the ingredients.

❹ Grease a 1 kg (2 lb) loaf tin and line it with baking parchment. Spoon the cake mixture in, levelling the top of the mixture once it is in the tin by tapping it sharply.

❺ Bake in the preheated oven for 55–60 minutes, or until a skewer inserted into the cake comes out clean.

❻ Leave to cool in the tin for 5 minutes. Turn out on to a wire rack and leave until completely cool. Cut into slices. This cake will keep for a few days in an air-tight container kept in a cool, dry place.

Simple Sherry Trifle

Preparation time: 10 minutes + 15 minutes cooling. Serves 3–4.

Although I have used a medium-dry sherry here, you can also make this with brandy or a sweet liqueur. The cheapest way to obtain these is to buy them in measures from the college bar (you need about 3 measures), if you live on campus.

a small raspberry-flavour swiss roll, cut into 8
    slices
2 bananas, sliced
6 tablespoons medium-dry sherry
2 tablespoons jam

74 g (3 oz) packet of custard mix
1 tablespoon single cream, plus extra to serve
chopped nuts, glacé cherries, silver balls or
    hundreds and thousands, to decorate

❶ Place the swiss roll slices and banana in the bottom of a serving bowl.

❷ Soak with the sherry, and spread the jam over the slices.

❸ Put the custard mix into a measuring jug and make up to 300 ml (½ pint) with boiling water.

❹ Mix the tablespoon of cream with the custard and pour over the trifle base. Level the surface and leave to cool for about 15 minutes.

❺ Before serving, decorate with your chosen topping.

Brioche and Butter Pudding

Preparation time: 5 minutes + 30 minutes cooking. Serves 2–4.

You can, of course, make this pudding with slices of bread. Since the time when I made this recipe with some brioche rolls that I had in the house, however, I have been a dedicated brioche and butter pudding fan. Instead of using marmalade, you can substitute your favourite jam, or even mincemeat.

2 brioche rolls
25–50 g (1–2 oz) butter
2 tablespoons marmalade

300 ml (½ pint) milk
2 eggs, beaten

❶ Preheat the oven to Gas Mark 4/ 180°C/350°F.

❷ Slice each roll into 5 pieces, and then butter each slice and place half of the slices in a pie dish. Cover with marmalade and top with the other brioche slices, butter-side up.

❸ Beat together the milk and eggs. Pour them over the brioche slices and push the slices down into the milk and egg mixture.

❹ Cook for 30–35 minutes, until well risen and brown.

Index